Also by r.h. Sin

Whiskey Words & a Shovel
Whiskey Words & a Shovel II
Whiskey Words & a Shovel III
Rest in the Mourning
A Beautiful Composition of Broken
Algedonic
Planting Gardens in Graves
Planting Gardens in Graves Volume Two
Planting Gardens in Graves Volume Three
She Felt Like Feeling Nothing
Empty Bottles Full of Stories
She Just Wants to Forget
Falling Toward the Moon
We Hope This Reaches You in Time
A Crowded Loneliness
She's Strong, but She's Tired
She Fits Inside These Words
Winter Roses after Fall
Dream, My Child
Anywho, I Love You
I Hope She Finds This
I Hope This Reaches Her in Time Revised Edition
Come Back to Me
This Day Is Dark
Beautiful Sad Eyes, Weary Waiting for Love
Ascending Assertion
A Midnight Moon
The Year of Letting Go
New Moons
My Dear Wildflower

SERENITY'S SONG

Serenity's Song
The Melody of Healing

r.h. Sin

Andrews McMeel
PUBLISHING®

Contents

Introduction ix

IN YOU, I FIND REFLECTION. 1

CALM IS THE CURE. 27

INTERLUDES: The Last Peace 45

○

Introduction

There is a deep and profound desire for harmony dwelling within your soul. Your heart has been through so much over the years, and now you're finally at this place where you truly understand what it is your heart requires to feel safe. You have always wanted to be open, vulnerable, and transparent, but the people you've invested energy into have often made you believe that you must wear a shield or build a wall in an attempt to protect yourself, and over the years, that same wall has also kept the right things from getting in as you'd go on to believe that what you desire most is nonexistent and can't be found in your lifetime. But I assure you that there is still at least one song worth listening to, and the melody within it will match the melody within your heart. You see, this song will be filled with all the elements you've been searching for, and from this, the harmony you've needed all this time will finally find its way into your heart.

So, let us begin to cultivate levels of serenity. Here, in this book, we prepare a place for the most harmonious love.

In You, I Find Reflection.

maybe it's the way the stars burn
in the night sky, just to watch her soul at rest
or how the sun follows her throughout the day
providing her with a personal spotlight
to highlight her importance here on this planet

tell her that she's beautiful
before that foundation meets her face
tell her she's magic on days when her soul
feels depleted and weary from trying to be
her best for everyone and everything

rub her feet at the end of the day
for she has traveled down many dark
and troubled paths just to get to this moment

give her your full attention
because being on the other side
of her heart expression
is a blessing that should be cherished
and the fact that she trusts you enough
to open up about what's going on in her head
is the most beautiful gift you'll ever receive

if you get the chance to love her before i do
do what it takes to hold her heart and
interest
because if you ever let her go
i'll do everything you couldn't do
i'll do everything i can to help her
forget that she was ever hurt by you

I want to apologize to you because, while I always knew that I could love you in the way you needed, I was distracted, investing my time and energy in spaces where love couldn't be appreciated. I sought out security from people who could not protect me. I've shared moments that meant nothing to the other person, but I guess, in truth, you only know they're the wrong person when it ends with your heart in pieces.

I think back to all the ways I've searched for you—navigating, constantly changing direction without a map, not even knowing what the destination would actually be. I've come to understand that healing those old wounds is the best way to welcome new love, and without that, one is destined to a cycle of disappointment.

I can tell you that I'm done replaying what happened; I'm done repeatedly settling for chaos when my deepest desire is peace. I'm done settling for places where you don't reside or with a heart that isn't yours. I know you're here with me, sharing this moment. I know that you understand everything I've expressed, because you've been there before. And now, I'm asking you to take my hand and let me walk beside you in love and peace. Let us begin to build our imperfect utopia on a foundation of trust, understanding, and healing.

In You, I Find Reflection.

I keep telling myself that maybe you're reading this right now, but it's like I can't be sure and yet I still want to try to reach you in this moment, to tell you that everything you've suffered and survived has meaning because everything that stood in your way has gone on to help you learn what you want, need, and deserve. You see, the troubles you've experienced turned out to be blessings as you made several discoveries of what to avoid; even more, those things motivated you to begin healing.

Sometimes healing can feel lonely, and there are days when you feel invisible to anything genuine or real, but right now, I see you, Love. I see your war-torn heart, and it's the most beautiful thing anyone could ever witness. I see into your tired eyes as you read this, and I see glimpses of a beautiful future, and I won't lie; I'm also imagining myself being seen by you.

Your heart has never really wavered, even when broken; even while in pieces, you've still found new and beautiful ways to cultivate deeper levels of strength, finding the inspiration to move forward in the midst of everything that should've kept you stuck. I sit here in deep thought about you and these abilities to make it happen, always against the greatest odds, and while I'm nearly rendered speechless, I must find the words, because you're worth it.

There is something truly remarkable about the way you've chosen to fight that feeling... you know, that urge to allow this world to turn you completely cold. There is something truly divine in the way you've stood up for yourself against the opposition. And right now, I come to you with love and peace. A gentle reminder of how special you are, even to me.

You feel that, don't you? A genuine love, a safe space for your heart. Thank you so much for arriving here and for taking me in. Thank you for showing up as your authentic self each and every day.

that remarkable woman is more than
what meets the eye

In You, I Find Reflection.

If you take the time to look beneath the surface, a depth of emotion and infinite energy will meet you there. Far too often, the eyes remain focused on the flower with no intent on celebrating the roots. She is more than what meets the eye. She is more than what most sight can comprehend. She is greater than anything the mind can imagine. You see, she is filled with boundless possibilities. There is no limitation on all that she has to offer, but in order to truly understand this, you must take the time to delve deeper. You must take every opportunity to truly look within her heart if she allows you to get that close. And you must be willing to prove that you are deserving of her magic by remaining consistent and forthcoming in your intentions and actions.

She is far more than what meets the eye, but you have to be committed to your inner self to truly see inside. A woman with depth requires you to be deep. She's not missing anything she's lost because she knows that the one who truly sees her won't lose her.

No matter how many times I get my heart broken, my belief in you never changes. My love and encouragement toward the woman reading this will never falter. When I look back on the totality of my life, women have played a key role in who I am and who I'm becoming, and so I'd like to take this time to acknowledge you and your light. Your ability to be kind, loving, nurturing, and brilliant in your presence is very inspiring to me. Your strength, will, and determination as you push forward and move closer to all things your heart has dreamed up are so beautiful to me.

And, as always, I thank you for taking the time to visit with me here.

In You, I Find Reflection.

There is a stillness in your eyes that I can't shake; a beautiful, haunting heaven is the only way to describe it. The dream of you lives somewhere deep within me, so much so that this idea of you has stitched itself into my mind. I've lied to myself in the past, minimizing this feeling to nothing more than a crush, but the weight of my desire has been heavy enough for me to finally admit the truth. And so I'm writing this here in hopes that it gets to you.

> SNOW ... on a Christmas day ...
> SUMMER after months of rain ...
> a lake in the desert
> a drip of water during a drought
> there's just something inside your existence
> that's been calling my heart out

What an incredible dream you are, the way you float through a fantasy built within a world of your own making, filled with harmony. There is an unapologetic beauty in the way you exist, courage in your heart, profound and deep. Your connection to nature, the ground beneath your feet, and the wind grasping for your skin for replenishment because somehow it knows that you are the source. You could move mountains if you wanted to. You could settle the sea with a thought.

Maybe you know this already, or maybe I've told you before, but I just can't help but desire to reach for you with words that feel like mirrors, reflecting everything that so many before me have not seen or failed to acknowledge.

I love it here, this place where we meet to share in this delight and craving for peace amid the noise. For a minute or two, we are suspended in a framework built on love and understanding. You feel me, and I see you.

There, of course, will be days when the world may weigh you down, moments when the people you trust may turn upon you, revealing their true motives, but you must always remember that it's not happening to you, it's happening for you, and while your world may face disruptions from time to time, remember these words. Remember this feeling.

In You, I Find Reflection.

I've felt so certain about your existence because if there are people in this world who set their sights on hurting others, then surely there is someone moving through the days with a deep sense of longing and desire to match the love given to them.

The thought of you wakes me up each morning, among other things. The day offers me the chance to love myself in a way that opens my heart to you, and with every passing moment, you are near—closer than before, the distance between us fading with every setting sun.

The night becomes a sort of capsule for our thoughts; sometimes, our minds are rendered restless as we think of one another. Fantastic fantasies cultivated by two souls meant to collide softly. You, a gentle reminder of everything I could ever want, and I like to think . . . the thought of me, of us, is somewhere deep beneath the surface of your heart.

I told the moon about this feeling of love for you sprouting out from my mind, my eyes fixated on this vision of utopia. My arms stretched out into darkness in search of your light. I can hear you calling out to me in song—a melody I once forgot, remembered only recently as time draws us near.

I am changed and transformed after all the things I've gone through, and I believe you are too. Our cycles of healing are somehow in sync as we prepare our hearts for recognition and remembrance of everything we were always meant to do . . . together.

I love the way you refused to give your ex the power to make you believe that you were asking for too much or the way you discovered that, by loving yourself, you give yourself permission to maintain a level of happiness that none of your partners have been able to respect or protect.

You found your light in the darkest hour. You pulled yourself through mud and still came out clean. I write this message to acknowledge the many ways you survived the things that kept you from your highest self.

I don't think it's too late for you, and I understand the fear of what you want not existing. If you stop for a moment to fully look upon your life, you will discover the many occasions when fear could not keep you from reaching the things you've wanted. Even this moment is a manifestation of your desire to mentally consume something that speaks to where you are and inspires you to keep going.

In You, I Find Reflection.

There was a point last year when the moon was so eager to get a glimpse of the sun that they stood perfectly in front of one another, a beautiful alignment considered rare to the occupants of Earth. And at that moment, I took my glasses off, the ones meant to protect my eyes from the solar eclipse, and for three seconds, three whole seconds that felt like a version of forever, I knew that, this year, I would find the one I'd been searching for. I knew at that moment that I would discover that perfect alignment that would one day astonish anyone observing that event.

I tell you this because I know you have begun to remember the ways in which we've done this before. Every version of us throughout the years split up with the understanding that, when the time was right, we'd reunite and carry out all of our soul missions.

I tell you this because I want your heart to smile, your soul to know that it has found its counterpart, and your mind at ease whenever it thinks of me.

I chase the night sky, my eyes fixated on the moon. I nearly grab the stars, dreaming of our love. You are a safe place, a profound belief. The most beautiful idea that God has ever had.

I think about the length of time I've gone without you, and while it used to bother my heart, I now understand the lessons that needed to be learned in the times we'd spent apart.

At any moment before, what I felt I deserved was unattainable because I didn't love myself enough. It just so happens that, on my way to a deeper respect for my own heart, I am now able to fully see you for who you are and what you'll mean to me.

Perhaps you'll read this and know how much my heart has longed to know what it means to be loved by someone like you. I know that, just like mine, your path to this moment has been painful and confusing, but what I offer here is a moment of clarity that can be infinite if you decide to accept it.

I feel that we both can love one another in a way that creates an unbreakable bond. Somehow I understand that you'll be the one to fully appreciate my love, a love that has been overlooked by everyone who came before you.

In You, I Find Reflection.

What a beautiful woman you are, the way you hold kindness in your heart and a space for love that resembles magic. I talk into the night air, hoping that my words reach the moon, for it is to be understood that the cosmos are familiar with your light. Your essence is born from nebulous stars; your existence is the galaxy's color. You've given me newfound hope and belief that all that I could ever need can be found in your presence. I've learned lessons and taken paths, wrong turns, and dead ends, but this moment is the one when I finally find the love of my life inside your soul. This shared moment when you are reading this with this voice inside your head.

I love you. I want you. I need you.

May the universe take our hands and guide them to one another, and my heart find its home at the touch of your fingertips.

There is something magnificent about a woman who sits at a frequency high above the negativity. Someone who has mastered the ability to emotionally regulate. Someone who understands what makes her happy because she's taken accountability for her own joy. She knows that she doesn't have to go outside of herself to find what she needs. She refuses to give in to the impulse to do something that could sabotage her life and her heart.

There is something so beautiful about the woman who has chosen to chase herself. She is in pursuit of love and knows that the love she requires can be found within her heart. There is something so magnetic about the woman who wants to discover more of her own soul because she knows that self-mastery will not only heal her wounds but also help her find her soul mate.

She speaks life into herself and into those who she cares for. She nurtures anything that is dependent on her essence. Her divine nature makes her rare and one of a kind, and she knows this—so much so that she refuses to waste her time and energy on things that do not align with her dreams or her purpose.

I love that woman for everything that others may have failed to appreciate. She loves herself, and it mirrors in the reflection of her everyday choices. She roots her decisions in a desire for peace, and I long to know every bit about who she is. I'd like to live forever in her heart. I need to know how it feels to be adored by her.

In You, I Find Reflection.

I imagine being chosen by heaven the moment you fall for me. I can hear a harp playing to us through these emotions in the distance. Clouds parting to show us the sun, gazing into the fire that reminds us of what we are cultivating, magic in every moment we connect.

I keep thinking about what it means to be loved by you, what it means to be loved by someone who has always dreamed of their energy and devotion being reciprocated. I keep thinking about the things that you had to face on your way to this moment and the realization that your heart is meant for magic and nothing less. I spend days searching for a quiet corner just so that I can fully process these ideas of you that live within my heart and head, and sometimes I wonder how you did it. How could someone so gentle and loving go to war and battle down the things put in place to destroy them? How does someone so kind defend themselves with all the energy they have and stand firm in the darkness, beneath a storm, with no real fear or not enough fear to make them change their mind about the love they deserve? But isn't that it? You have been unwavering in your desire and longing. You have confronted every aspect of your heartbreak because you believe in the part of you that is capable of real love, and so you know that this love exists because you've maintained the courage to give it.

And I guess I just want to be the one who matches that fire. I'll be honest: I have loved love, and that has gotten me into trouble. You see, everything you are, I have searched for that in everyone who was never meant to be you, but I arrive here wiser, stronger, healed in the deepest of ways because of all the times my love was unappreciated. I arrive here in this moment, different, changed by sadness and disappointment. I was led to you by letting go. I am closer to your heart with each passing day.

In You, I Find Reflection.

she's like the moon, steady in her phases
powerful enough to move oceans

in every wave of her silence
you could hear
the gentle whispers of God

IN YOU, I FIND REFLECTION.

she wore the night sky
like a dress
every star
a story of self-love
courage and magic

her heart, an ocean
a mysterious depth
with a pull as strong
as the tides

In You, I Find Reflection.

her soul dances with the moon
a glow in the darkness
a brilliant guiding light

you missed it
the galaxies in her eyes
you lost it
the love in her heart
you took her for granted
you fumbled the world

In You, I Find Reflection.

She's a cosmic siren.

i see God in her eyes
i hear angels in her voice
and the scars on her heart
tell a story of how
she went to war
with her demons and won

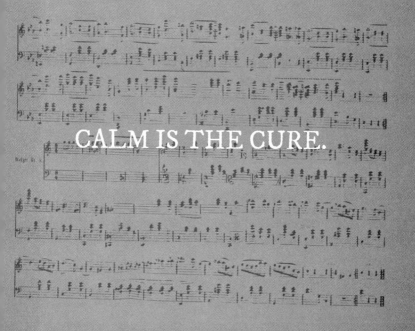

CALM IS THE CURE.

I'm discovering the power of remaining calm and doing inner work. The power of acceptance and forgiveness. It's these things, these daily practices, that have helped me in my writing and in my expression. My art feels as if it caters to you and you alone because I've been going to this place, this deep place of self-love, and it is furthering my understanding of all things, especially love, and how we interact with it. I've gone through some things, but in those things, I have discovered the most beautiful lessons. I'm ascending, and I hope that when you read these words, you feel that way and learn what is needed to raise your frequency and taste level in regard to the way you live and the love you search for.

I feel so empowered by all the things that were meant to break me. I feel so inspired by your ability to arrive here in search of something more, something deeper. Thank you for giving me the opportunity to speak to you and to speak to your heart.

Calm Is the Cure.

I often find it difficult to be angry for an extended amount of time, and today is one of those days when I am once again asking myself... what is that, or why is that? When I came into this year, I had decided to give myself permission to genuinely feel the things I am feeling in the moment, and in those observations, I find myself processing those emotions and then deciding that they aren't worth impacting my entire day or my life.

With time, this has gotten so much easier. I'm not perfect in my observation of a feeling because there are times when I react to the emotion felt, but after maybe 30 or so minutes, I just can't find it in me to be upset anymore, and I revert back to a peace that leads back to this blissful state. While I wouldn't necessarily say I like being triggered, it's also nice to know what works for me at that moment so that, next time, I can completely ignore the other person.

It also helps to remember that the people who want to trigger you aren't real people. What I mean is that they don't exist in the way you and I do. Their inability to regulate themselves pushes them to try and trigger others to help with their own insecurities, and maybe I find myself back to laughter because it's actually funny to think that I could completely waste a day on someone who doesn't even value theirs.

I've been residing in this space of deep gratitude. There is something so intriguing about finding beauty, even amid a chaotic moment or day. This mindset has helped me cultivate a profound love for myself and all the good things in my life. The moment I decide to look deeply, whether it be inward or at my surroundings, I find a source of joy in understanding that, in this life, I will continuously lose what I shouldn't keep to make room for more of what I desire.

Shift your focus today, even as things get harder. Focus on what makes you feel good and what brings you joy. Give energy to those little moments of peace, because they will always outweigh the times of noise and conflict. This is more obvious in the long run. I look back on everything I thought was wrong, and there are times when I laugh to myself because those things became stepping-stones to something better.

Calm Is the Cure.

Where love used to make me anxious, my nervous system now feels safe. I think in the past I mistook the feeling of wasps roaming inside my chest as butterflies. In the end, it was always true. My body registered danger way before the relationship turned toxic.

I can only ever focus on one heart in the matter of attraction. The games, the juggling of many, and the urge to entertain several have never intrigued me. My biggest flex is that where you might have felt neglected and overlooked in your previous interactions, with me, you feel seen, important, and valued. I listen . . . I listen with my heart and soul. And so I begin to comprehend you deeply. My gaze, my interest, and my intention are all based on this desire to uplift you. My intention is rooted in a pure place that allows me to appreciate everything you are beneath the surface.

And not everyone wants this type of attention. In contrast, I deem this the right approach. I have discovered that I am not for everyone, those times when my focus was on the heart and when my nature of being considerate and selfless have rendered me alone and unappreciated. And while I used to get upset about it, I now understand that not everyone is ready for the type of love they claim to dream about. You see, there are many people who say what they want, but their actions prove otherwise, and the saddest part of it all is that they continue a cycle in which they ultimately end up alone. That or they settle for everything that is nothing in the end.

But we're not talking about them; let us refocus on you. The years of mistrust and devotion invested in the wrong places. The lies you know after sharing your heart with fraudulent individuals. The heartbreak did not necessarily destroy your need for real love. In fact, the pitfalls of dating have made you wiser. The red flags are more apparent, and what your heart requires has been somewhat inspired by all the moments that never lived up to their potential. You had to get what you didn't want in order to know what you genuinely needed, and so you'll know when it's right for you because you learned what isn't.

With my heart fixated and focused on you, I get the opportunity to know what you need. The way you want your peace to be respected and protected. The way you require love to be deep and gentle. You want to be in a relationship that isn't a battlefield. You're tired of compromising

CALM IS THE CURE.

your joy for unnecessary conflict, and while you're strong enough to go it alone, you do want someone who you can lean on or depend on during the most difficult seasons of your life. You're a giver, and most of what you've known are takers who didn't even deserve you in the first place, and so what your heart craves is a lover who is willing to match the way you devote yourself to the relationship.

You have no desire to compete for one's attention, nor do you want to share someone with someone else when you know that you deserve it all because you're worth everything. Your loyalty requires that you be with someone who is transparent. Your ability to articulate yourself just means that you want to be with someone who can process and communicate their feelings. And in this world, where people are constantly entertaining temporary nothings, you want something that'll last.

You're not asking for too much. What you want exists, and I know this because I have always been ready to give these things even though it hasn't always been appreciated. I still have so much of this to offer, and I'm not alone in that, and you don't have to feel alone in your relationships. No, you don't need to settle when there is someone out there who will love you in all the ways you need. Whenever you lose hope and need a reminder, find a mirror and stare into the truth. Real love exists because it has lived inside of you, and while you might have given it to the wrong person, your love replenishes itself.

I end this by thanking you for upholding your ideas of love. People like us are built for one another, and you are the real reason that I still believe in true love, because, no matter what you've gone through, you've remained true, Love.

There's a beautiful kindness residing inside you. I think there are times when you feel like you should bury it, but I'm happy you decided against that. Kindness provides a sturdy foundation for love, and your love is the most valuable of all. And so I see no reason why anyone in your past should have the power to compromise your desire to share that part of yourself with the right person.

Too often, your instinct to be softer with your beloved had been met with mistreatment. And so after all those moments of hurt, it's natural that you begin to see this part of you as a weakness, but even so, you always find your way back to who you truly are, and I'm just hoping you never change.

Kindness is a lost art, something you've managed to create, be, and sustain through everything you've gone through. Kindness is a bridge, an extension into a world where bliss exists. It's just that sometimes you have to go through hardship to discover a place where your kindness will be appreciated, and something tells me that you're close.

I say this because you've reached a point in your life when you've been doing the work. You've taken the time to process all the hurt you've experienced, and you have taken the initiative to forgive those who have hurt you. This is the beginning of discovering a love that won't require you to regret being kind.

I have a soft spot in my heart for those who embody an unbreakable kindness. To me, that part of one's character is a beautiful strength, and so I am writing this for you. I pay homage to the softness in your heart and your ability to be gentle with others, and I wish you nothing but the best as you move through this world in hopes of finding your soul mate.

CALM IS THE CURE.

Something we often overlook is the way others treat themselves. It's important to understand that if a person is okay with destroying their own life, they'll have no problem with implementing measures to disrupt yours. This becomes even more vital in friendship and romantic relationships. This is not to cast judgment upon others, but it is simply a tool that must be utilized to prevent unnecessary damage and harm to oneself.

This concept may be more difficult to understand in our youth because being young comes with its own difficulties of existing, and maybe these words are only for those who are mature enough to process everything written here. Maybe these words will only really matter to anyone who is currently going through a situation in which another person has decided to rain down a sort of terror in an attempt to disrupt whatever peace could have been cultivated.

Seek out connections rooted in calm persistence, spaces that feel like solitude even as shared with that other person. Look to creating bonds with those who embody the type of character worthy of your trust and energy. These are the things that have helped me maintain my peace of mind. If you want to experience beautiful relationships, pursue only those who treat themselves beautifully.

I have no desire to be here in this place, and the most beautiful thing I ever did was refuse to allow my desire to leave a part of my life to also mean that I want to leave my life in general. I think we make decisions over the course of our lives that, at some point, no longer line up with the person we've become, and when you deny yourself the urge to leave, you find yourself in a deep depression, a profound sadness that causes the sort of emptiness that makes you believe that ending your life is a reasonable choice. But with time, you discover that you can end a part of your life and still continue to live.

That's where I'm at in my journey. I don't want to be in spaces I've outgrown. I don't want to reside or take up space in someone's life that has no real room for me. I'm not one of those people who feel like they have ownership over others, and so I'm always looking forward to detaching from a thing, a place, or a relationship that isn't aligned with the direction I'm heading in, as far as my heart and soul.

Starting over is a gift, especially to those of us who no longer feel comfortable, safe, or at peace with where we've been. And I hope you find the courage to write this new chapter for yourself. I believe that the fear of being alone keeps us repeating a dreadfully worn-out version of existence. We bury so much of what our future can be just to entertain places that feel familiar, but it's time for something new. It's time to pave a different path, one that resembles everything we've seen in our dreams.

After years of tension, walking on eggshells, and protecting the ego of those who have been the biggest perpetrators of the chaos in my life, I realized during moments of self-love and reflection that love itself does not have to feel like a war and that your home should never feel like a battlefield. And so it is my hope that, as you read these words, you are inspired to cultivate the peace you deserve.

CALM IS THE CURE.

I'm a lover of peace, and so I give silence to spaces that cause me to compromise the harmony in my heart. I think it's important to protect that part of you. I think it's vital that you reclaim your energy, time, and power by refusing to invest it where you feel drained, confused, and hurt.

Life isn't perfect, but you can cultivate safer spaces where your heart can evolve, your mind can expand, and your soul can flourish.

I'm saying this because I genuinely care. I've been so focused on my peace lately that it has led me to put more distance between myself and things that don't align with the direction of my spirit or the vibrations of my soul. I hope you do the same for yourself, because you are worthy of love and peace.

To the woman who is reclaiming her time, heart, and love from places that failed to appreciate her presence, I hope you understand that you're on the right path as you heal those old wounds, making room for self-love and preparing your future to be beautiful and prosperous. To the woman reading this right now, I am genuinely inspired by the way you shine, and I adore your light as your eyes wander gently through what's been written here. You are incredible, you are magic, and you deserve the softest version of love. I know you'll walk into all the places that align with you because you refuse to give up or settle, and so these words are for you and only you.

CALM IS THE CURE.

My heart is with anyone who has had their love overlooked by someone they considered a future with. I know it isn't easy to process the end of a relationship you believed would last a lifetime, but it's important to note that what's meant to be will be, and what no longer deserves your energy will leave you so that you can find something better. In the end, you must begin to love yourself and heal. You must understand that your most remarkable love story has yet to be written, and the moment you move on is the moment you pick up a pen to write it.

I've imagined love to be this gentle place for so many years of my life, and yet, even as I imagine it to feel like home, I've spent the majority of my time dwelling in places that never really aligned with the future I saw for my heart. It's a terrible thing, the task of holding up a vision that at times feels impossible to cultivate. And still, throughout the heartbreak and disappointment, I still hang on to this hope, this need, this love for greater love, and I think we both have that in common.

I think, as you've read this book, you've gained not only a deeper understanding of what is written here but you've also been self-reflecting on your own journey, and there's a large part of you who is ready to embrace the soft parts of life. Inside you lives this desire for deep calm, security, and peacefulness. I believe that the first step to getting everything you deserve is to begin to pull back your energy from everything and everyone who has pushed you into the darkness, the chaos, and the noise. You're almost there, and I'm so proud of you.

CALM IS THE CURE.

There is a peace that awaits you; it lives in those silent moments of meditation. There is a joy that is yours; it lives behind whatever has been distracting you or obstructing your view of the present. I think it can be excruciating to find yourself lost, but there is a beautiful freedom in those who master the art of wandering through this world.

And I want nothing more than for you to discover this gift I've found, this beautiful path I've wandered onto. I think, more than ever, the world is split into two spaces, and there are many of us who, despite the pain we've felt, have either managed to hold on to our light or refuse to let it be completely extinguished. I want you to remember who you are and what you've survived. I want you to understand that you have shown great courage and ability in your navigation of this world and its troubles. I want you to know that you should never give up on yourself, because you've proven to be a strong and resourceful warrior. Good things are coming.

There is so much power and freedom in taking accountability for the ways you might have been wrong, even while being wronged by the other person. I think when I used to believe that you had to get a person back whenever they hurt you, this was usually in the form of arguing back and being dragged into a low-vibration situation, despite my best efforts. I discovered that when you give in, you give that person the opportunity to make you out to be someone you are not. And I know it's not easy, and it can feel like you're giving in to their bullshit, but the truth is, you don't have to hurt them just because you're getting hurt. You can just observe the way you're being treated, acknowledge the way you feel, and then silently decide what to do next.

Calm Is the Cure.

There has been a change within you, and not everyone can see it, but that's fine. These parts . . . the new parts of who you are, aren't meant to be experienced by those who are and will be left behind in the wake of your complete transformation.

Give yourself credit for how far you've come, and know that, with each passing day, you are closer to the most beautiful of all destinations—a place of self-love and reassurance, a place where all your dreams become real.

WHEN YOU'RE IN A HEALTHY RELATIONSHIP,
DISAGREEMENTS DO NOT BECOME WARS.

INTERLUDES: THE LAST PEACE

Loving a narcissist is like pouring liquid into a cup with no bottom. And it's only until you realize that they deserve none of what you have to offer that you can finally redirect the flow back into your own cup.

I LEVELED AND DISCOVERED PEACE WHEN I FOCUSED ON CHANGING MY REACTION INSTEAD OF TRYING TO CHANGE THE NARCISSIST.

INTERLUDES: THE LAST PEACE

CLEAN HEARTS ARE WINNING. GOOD
THINGS ARE BEGINNING TO HAPPEN FOR
GOOD PEOPLE. AFTER YEARS OF DROUGHT,
THE RAIN HAS COME TO CLEANSE YOU.

DECIDE THE KIND OF LIFE YOU WANT,
THEN DETACH FROM ANYONE WHO WANTS
YOU TO COMPROMISE THAT DREAM.

Interludes: The Last Peace

Just don't judge her by her worst days. In totality, that woman is always magic. She is always love, and even when things get dark, she discovers new and beautiful ways to shine.

Don't argue; just say "okay."

Interludes: The Last Peace

Just because her wins aren't loud
doesn't mean she's losing.

This is your era of attracting
the most beautiful things.

INTERLUDES: THE LAST PEACE

no drama
nothing toxic
calm aura
self-love
and healing

RECOGNIZING AND CURING
YOUR OWN TOXIC TRAITS
IS THE BIGGEST FLEX.

Interludes: The Last Peace

I just can't be bothered by anything or anyone standing in the way of my peace of mind.

in truth, i felt you
before i knew your name
like whispers written in the stars
like a song only my soul could comprehend

i would fall from heaven
just to sit in your presence
i'd trade eternity for the curve of your smile
for the way your eyes cause gravity to forget me

even if the world never sees us
even if time is for some reason unkind

i would choose you in every life
a stranger or my soul mate
a fleeting moment or forever

Interludes: The Last Peace

Through every moment of heartbreak, every setback, moments when the world attempted to dim your light, you have always burned brighter. You go from being a survivor to a brilliant force. A woman who knows that peace is not given but created . . . and healing is not waiting but deciding to go inward to practice self-love. Queen, your story is not written by the ones who tried to break you but by the way you continue to rise. Over and over again.

You know what... she has been the kind of woman who gave without keeping score, someone who has loved even when it hurt. She's been the woman who has stayed longer than she should have, hoping and believing, breaking down beneath the weight of unmet expectations, but she was never the problem. The ones she loved weren't ready for the kind of energy she carried.

She's done waiting to be seen by those too blind to appreciate her essence, presence, and worth. She finally sees herself, and that's enough.

INTERLUDES: THE LAST PEACE

Listen, I just wanted to say that you are not the brokenness they left behind. You are very much a storm that has learned to calm itself, the fire that refused to be extinguished. I want to remind you that healing isn't linear, but every step you take forward, even the smallest one, is a victory worthy of a beautiful celebration. You have survived many nights that have been darker than your doubts, and you have risen time and time again each morning with a heart brave enough to continue thriving. In truth, you are proof that pain can't bury beauty and that, even when love doesn't stay, you remain whole. Please, keep choosing yourself. You are the greatest love story you'll ever write, and the best chapters are yet to come.

It's strange the way you found the keys to unlock my light and my dark. The way you folded my pain gently and put me at ease. The way your heart ignited mine was just enough to remind me that love was necessary and possible.

INTERLUDES: THE LAST PEACE

Queen, the weight of your story sits in your bones, but it doesn't bend or break you. You carry both the tenderness and the ache, honoring each as part of the woman you are becoming. Even in silence, your spirit hums, a melody only those who've known both suffering and softness could ever understand.

You are not defined by the chaos that tried to consume you but by the grace with which you reclaimed yourself. Rooted and reaching. Soft but unshakable. You are proof that beauty can grow even in the darkest of places.

Refusing to repeat that cycle
is the greatest form
of self-love.

INTERLUDES: THE LAST PEACE

she's letting go
she's ending toxic cycles
she's saying no to anything
that compromises
her nervous system
she's just making room
for the healed version of herself

full of love
but mindful
of who i trust

Interludes: The Last Peace

she went confidently
into any struggle
because the pressure
only made her a diamond

This is the era during which she sheds the weight of the lies so that she can rise in her truth.

Interludes: The Last Peace

Don't you see, my love, you're like the moon. You shine brighter during your darkest hour.

Eventually, the scars turn into armor.
You heal those wounds to protect
your heart from further damage.

INTERLUDES: THE LAST PEACE

SHE WASN'T BROKEN; SHE WAS
JUST BREAKING FREE.

Her light is fierce; her soul is magic.

Interludes: The Last Peace

Don't you see? Your heartbreak was not an ending; it was your becoming.

And in the end, she took back every piece
of herself that they tried to erase.

Interludes: The Last Peace

The storms only made her wild; the calm made her strong and wise.

SHE TURNED HER TEARS INTO RIVERS,
LEADING TO NEW WORLDS.

Interludes: The Last Peace

The goddess within her soul had never left; it was just waiting to be called upon.

Her self-love became a sword,
slicing through the lies.

Interludes: The Last Peace

A woman reclaiming her power remembers her magic and creates her own paradise.

That discomfort you feel is an inner awakening. You are transforming and growing. This is a moment of evolution. Pay attention to the way you feel, and be patient with yourself.

Interludes: The Last Peace

Healing will often require you to sever ties with people you thought you needed because, as you begin to patch up those wounds, your stomach will turn at the thought of loving people who are responsible for all the things you had to fix.

Remarkable woman, you've been through so much in your life, and you've held so much in your heart. You've found yourself placed in front of obstacles that could never stop you, unnecessary wars during which you came out victorious. I write this in acknowledgment of all that you are and everything you've survived. You arrive at this moment scarred but healing, weary but made of magic.

Interludes: The Last Peace

Why settle for a relationship that resembles a nightmare when, right now, there is someone in this world dreaming about what it would feel like to be with someone like you . . .

When you are no longer triggered into feelings you don't want, that's peace.

Interludes: The Last Peace

She didn't respond because she's at peace with your absence, and you'll never get another chance to waste her time again.

THIS IS MY ERA TO BE UNBOTHERED BY ALL
THE THINGS YOU USED TO DO TO TRIGGER ME.

Interludes: The Last Peace

Letting go meant making room
for better experiences.

Keep healing, Queen; healthy looks good on you.

INTERLUDES: THE LAST PEACE

LOVING SOMEONE WHO UNDERSTANDS
THE CONCEPT OF EMOTIONAL REGULATION
IS A TOP-TIER EXPERIENCE.

Stay soft, but only share it with those who deserve that gentle part of you.

INTERLUDES: THE LAST PEACE

ONCE SHE DISCOVERS THE PEACE IN
UPGRADING EVERY PART OF HER LIFE,
SHE'LL LET YOU GO FOR GOOD.

Things are aligning for you even in your darkest hours. Trust it; claim this.

Interludes: The Last Peace

The things you've lost weren't necessary for this moment or your future. Accept that the best is yet to come and that you are exactly where you should be.

I JUST DON'T HAVE TIME FOR
TEMPORARY PEOPLE, SMALL SURFACE
CONVERSATIONS, AND DRAMA.

Interludes: The Last Peace

Stop reacting. Observe it, and if it's not aligned with you, move on.

You're amazing on a soul level. My condolences to whoever lost you.

INTERLUDES: THE LAST PEACE

MORE AND MORE, I'M BECOMING
CONFIDENT ABOUT THE LOVE I DESERVE,
AND THIS IS WHY I REFUSE TO SETTLE.

A CALM WOMAN IS ROOTED IN A CLARITY
THAT ALLOWS HER TO SEE THROUGH YOUR
BULLSHIT EVEN BEFORE YOU SPEAK.

Interludes: The Last Peace

This year, you cried, you learned, and you healed. Next year, you thrive and enjoy fully all the things you've been manifesting.

I GET IT; YOU'VE BEEN TRYING TO FIND
YOURSELF IN OTHER PEOPLE, BUT YOU'RE RARE.

Interludes: The Last Peace

Cool, calm. I am reclaiming my power.

Growing, thriving, and vibing in silence.

INTERLUDES: THE LAST PEACE

IT'S BEAUTIFUL HOW SHE OWNS THE STRENGTH
AND BRILLIANCE IN HER SOFTNESS.

There is something beautiful awaiting you in the inside of your heart. When you have that desire for love, please, by all means, venture inward, because you are capable of giving yourself everything that others refuse to.

INTERLUDES: THE LAST PEACE

EVERYTHING ABOUT HER FEELS LIKE LOVE, AND I THINK THAT'S WHY SHE'S CHOSEN TO BE SINGLE: SHE KNOWS THAT THE RIGHT RELATIONSHIP WILL NOT COMPROMISE THE PEACE SHE'S CULTIVATED ON HER OWN.

Eventually, the woman you took for granted will figure out that you were the thing that was blocking her blessings.

Interludes: The Last Peace

She's changing for the better, expanding her soul's essence, and taking up space. She has found her voice and the courage to detach from anything or anyone who isn't aligned with the peace she craves, and if you fumble her, you'll never get another chance.

that woman took heartbreak
and transformed it into an awakening

Interludes: The Last Peace

Give me moon gazing and sunsets with a lover who calms my nervous system.

Serenity's Song

she's good for the soul
she's good for the mind
she's good for the future

INTERLUDES: THE LAST PEACE

THIS IS THE ERA OF UNDERSTANDING THAT
LOVE NEEDS ACTIONS AND THAT APOLOGIES
REQUIRE A CHANGE IN BEHAVIOR.

she's learning how to be better to herself
self-love is her superpower

Interludes: The Last Peace

The more you heal, the happier you become, the more you understand that seeking revenge isn't necessary.

i let you go because this is my era
of surrounding myself with winners

Interludes: The Last Peace

Queen, you are essential
if they don't prioritize you, let them go

i love being alone, but i'm meant
for deep companionship

Serenity is finally understanding that the person who went out of their way to hurt me was never my person and that their decision to let me down was also their acceptance of never making it to the bigger picture of what my life can and will become.

Serenity, for me, was the discovery of a lie, a betrayal that would go on to help me pave a path of healing, processing, and self-love. A path that would eventually lead me back to myself with a new and profound understanding that I am the source and that everything I need resides deep within my own heart.

Serenity is accepting that there are people who will play themselves out of a position in your life and that you must let them go so that you can fill your life with healthier things in their absence; as time goes on, those people will sometimes understand how badly they destroyed their own lives while trying to hurt you.

Serenity is allowing karma to do the job, refusing to allow your heart to hold a grudge or seek revenge for people who were never really worthy of your energy in the first place.

You've chosen peace, and I'm so proud of you for choosing yourself. Yes, I'm so proud of us.

Serenity's Song copyright © 2025 by r.h. Sin. All rights reserved.
Printed in the United States of America. No part of this book may
be used or reproduced in any manner whatsoever without written
permission, except in the case of reprints in the context of reviews.

The authorised representative in the EEA is Simon and Schuster
Netherlands BV, Herculesplein 96 3584 AA Utrecht, Netherlands.
(info@simonandschuster.nl)

Andrews McMeel Publishing
a division of Andrews McMeel Universal
1130 Walnut Street, Kansas City, Missouri 64106

www.andrewsmcmeel.com

25 26 27 28 29 KPR 10 9 8 7 6 5 4 3 2 1

ISBN: 979-8-8816-0018-1

Library of Congress Control Number: 2025933722

Editor: Patty Rice
Assistant Editor: Danys Mares
Art Director: Diane Marsh
Production Editor: Elizabeth A. Garcia
Production Manager: Shona Burns

ATTENTION: SCHOOLS AND BUSINESSES

Andrews McMeel books are available at quantity discounts with
bulk purchase for educational, business, or sales promotional use.
For information, please email the Andrews McMeel Publishing
Special Sales Department: sales@andrewsmcmeel.com.